How some retailers make more money than others

Paul Watkins & Diego Boniolo

Published by Paul Watkins Ltd
PO Box 12082 Hamilton, 3248, New Zealand
paul@paulwatkins.co.nz
www.howsomeretailers.com

Cover Designed by VB Designs www.vbdesigns.com.au
Quotes are with the permission of those people quoted

First published 2010

ISBN 978-0-473-17873-4

To our understanding families

CONTENTS

"The mass market is dying. There is no longer one best song or one best kind of coffee. Now there are a million micro markets, but each micro market still has a BEST. If your micro market is 'organic markets in Tulsa', then that's your world. And being the best in THAT world is the place to be."

Seth Godin, marketer, speaker and author

Paul Watkins & Diego Boniolo

Introduction
How to make more money in retail

Making money out of retail can be hard work. You have huge overheads in the form of rent, staff wages, advertising and inventory. Generating enough gross profit to pay your expenses is not easy when all around you national chains are offering the same products at lower prices, a bigger range and spend millions on advertising.

Is there still a place for the smaller independent retailer? Even as part of a franchise chain, the issues of generating a good enough gross profit remain.

There is no silver bullet that will make a dramatic difference, but rather a series of processes, ideas and practices that if followed, will collectively improve your store's performance.

This book explains how you can grow your store's performance at very little cost. It explains how growing the gross profit starts with understanding the formula. The ideas are based on the personal observations by the authors of what works and what doesn't. Share the book with your team and treat it as a reference book.

Paul Watkins & Diego Boniolo

Chapter 1

Just when you reckon you got it worked out, the market changes

The 1-2-3 of retailing

To grow a retail business, you need a constant stream of customers, each of them spending the maximum you believe you can get out of them and each of them leaving with a desire to come back. Sounds so simple, but clearly there is a bit more to it.

What is your strategy for attracting more customers? What keeps your name alive in the minds of the target market in your community? What is your strategy for growing the customer spend? What are you actively doing to have them come back more often? How do you differ from your immediate competitors, including the Internet,. Should you be on the Internet yourself? These are the questions this book will answer in easy-to-implement, low or no-cost ways.

Since that category is failing, let me add another (failing) category

Marketer Seth Godin's blog dated March 7th 2008, says:

> "I drove past a hobby shop yesterday... the (sign on the) awning said, 'Hobby Shop, Trains, R/C Models, Coffee, Lottery.' Bit by bit, on each declining day, it became easier to become more average, to add one more item, to sell a few more lottery tickets or another cup of coffee. And then, the next thing you know, there are some dusty model trains in the back and you're running a convenience store. This place, just about every place, has a shot at greatness, at becoming a destination, a place with profits and happiness and growth. Along the way, it's easy to start compromising your marketing, because it seems like in that moment, its expedient."

Specialist stores work! Generalist stores don't! The trend around the world is for retail to go in two directions: big box retailers and small highly specialised stores staffed with 'experts'. The first offer a huge range at significant discounts or on very attractive terms such as 40 months to pay with no interest. The specialist store on the other hand can ask much higher prices, but the extra cost for goods must include expert advice and outstanding service.

You cannot be both – you MUST decide which one you want to be and your entire strategy must reflect this.

Just because it worked 5 years ago...

What has changed in the past 5 years? Technology? Social behaviour? Debt levels? Shopping patterns? Jobs? The age of the population? YES to all of these. The internet is here to stay as is texting and social media. The population is unquestionably ageing and we live considerably longer.

Malls had a boom time for a while, apparently now being surpassed in some countries by so-called 'super centers'. Do small suburban strip shopping centers have a future? Will all shopping be done on the internet? Will the category-killing big box retail chains dominate? Will franchised chains of specialist shops kill the true independent store?

We don't have a crystal ball, so it's impossible to answer these questions, but one thing is very clear to us. The smaller independent retailer CAN survive, but only if they understand the changing trading environment and alter their offer, image and most importantly, their customer relationship process.

"I remember when..."

We hear that a lot. We make no apology for our response, which is to get over it. Those times are gone forever and making the same money as before now requires a different mindset. On the positive side, it's not expensive to make the changes, but it is a little more labor intensive. The good news here, is that much of this can be outsourced.

Using price – but not as you imagine

Examples of price leadership are particularly apparent in retail. In every market there will be a price leader – someone that has a deliberate strategy of undercutting the others. They may not say 'cheapest' or 'lowest price', but be a little more subtle, using terms like 'affordable' and 'why pay more than you should?' This is a very difficult position to maintain as in every market there is someone who will under-price you on the pretext of a foot in the door, or generating cash flow or some other illogical reason.

Some stores deliberately price items at below cost to act as a draw card. An example is a big box retailer offering photo prints at 10cents, which is below the actual cost of the printed item. But to the stores, this is a marketing cost. Most stores like this are destination stores. This means that they are separated from malls and customers have to deliberately drive to them and not just happen to be walking by.

The theory is that if a customer has taken the time to go there, they will also browse the entire store and buy other high profit lines. Smaller specialty stores must use the opposite strategy, as we will discuss.

The $5 milkshake

Sometimes raising your price to well above those of your competition can work in your favor. It creates desire, anticipation, perceived quality and snob value.

In the movie Pulp Fiction, John Travolta is sitting in the restaurant with Uma Thurman and she orders a milkshake that costs $5. (Assume a normal price of less than $1). Travolta is stunned that a shake can cost that much and says "I gotta know what a $5 shake tastes like". He sips it and then proclaims, "It's a pretty f***ing good milkshake". Is it five times as good as a normal one? Of course not, but his anticipation of one costing that much and tasting much better is such that it must be. There is a clue in this for specialist retailers.

"We pride ourselves on our service"

"Service" has to be the most clichéd, overused and abused word in business today. It's made worse by nonsensical slogans such as 'Service is our middle name' and 'Our service is our difference'. And what must be the worst of all, 'Service with attitude'. These are all meaningless drivel and completely useless in terms of driving sales, but service is without doubt a competitive advantage if it is understood.

'Good service' is NOT a competitive edge

Why don't you tip every waiter? Many research studies show that restaurant guests do NOT tip for efficient speedy service. Incredibly they tip slow and inefficient service just as well. How come?

It turns out that we tip when we are made to feel special. Smiles, a joke, a little touch, pleasant conversation and taking what appears to be a genuine interest in the customer earns much higher tips than having the food delivered on time. A standout reason for tipping waiters was discovered to be remembering the customer from a previous visit.

So what are the lessons here? Things like being pleasant are not 'good service', they are fundamental good manners. But asking how a customer's husband is, because you remembered that last time they mentioned he was ill, or complimenting them on their clothing can constitute service that deserves a tip and massive loyalty.

The key

Is being an 'expert' to the customer. Positioning yourself as the 'expert' by asking why they want an item or what it is for, allows you to make recommendations.

What do you want to be famous for?

You can focus can be on a geographical area (e.g. like a dairy or pharmacy), a specific service (e.g. being a guru on taking great photographs), a specific market segment (e.g. teen girls between 13 and 18), a type of customer (e.g. young mums) or a single product range (e.g. cell phones).

If you really want to grow your business, this is the biggie in terms of bang-for-buck. This is usually the most successful of all the strategies. This is because it leads to you being the big fish in the market by reducing the size of the pond.

Chapter 2
The critical retail formula for growth

The retail profit formula

Understanding what drives your retail profits is the key to successful retailing. It's all in the retail formula:

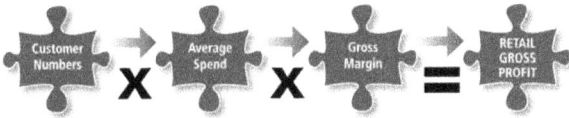

You must have a strategy for each one of these three factors, which is what the rest of this book deals with. You should set targets for each of these. For example, you may want 100 customers a day, each spending $40, with a gross margin on each item sold of 45%. That would be a gross profit of:

100 customers x $40 spend x 0.45 margin = $1,800

The $1,800 is the money you pay the wages, rent, advertising and all other expenses from. It is very important to share these targets with your team as they must also appreciate that their wages come from these numbers.

When one is down, emphasis should be placed on the other two

If customer count is down, gross profits can usually be maintained by placing greater emphasis on the other two factors.

For example, if the customer count has dropped from 100 to 80 per day, then putting greater emphasis on ways to raise the average spend per customer from $40 to $50. This will result in:

80 customers x $50 spend x 0.45 margin = $1,800

So the dollar profit is maintained. However, it is a frequently noticed mistake that when retailers see a falling customer count, they lower prices to get customers back. Let's see the impact on the formula of this strategy: It may bring the customer numbers back to 100 per day, but as items have been discounted, the average spend could drop to $35 and the gross margin to 40%. The overall impact is therefore:

100 customers x $35 spend x 0.40 margin = $1,400

You are far worse off this way and putting prices back up is not easy as customers now expect discounted prices. Each of the next three sections will cover these three factors in depth, that is, growing the customer count, growing the average customer spend and growing (or at least maintaining) the gross margin on items sold.

Benchmarking your numbers

What are the averages for your specific industry? If you do not have software or industry reports to compare yourself to, ask the supplier's reps. They should have a good knowledge of averages such as customer numbers, average customer spend and gross margins. You must know these so you can set realistic targets.

SMART targets, slightly redefined

On the subject of setting targets you will have all heard of 'SMART' targets. Here is the best way to use this concept when setting your targets for this formula:

S PECIFIC

Well defined targets and clearly understood by everyone

M EASURABLE

Can be measured daily, weekly or monthly

A GREED UPON

The entire team must agree to them, not just be told. If the team collectively comes up with them, the commitment to achieve them is huge

R EALISTIC

This is where benchmarking comes in

T IME BOUND

To be achieved by a specific date

The most critical line is AGREED UPON. If you let you're your team help set targets they almost always get achieved.

Publish the results at least weekly on the staff notice board. It is a huge mistake to be precious about these. You are not giving them NET profit, just the gross retail profit that all costs including their wages must come from. Involving the whole team always produces better results.

Chapter 3
Driving customer numbers

Filling your shop

Some years ago I listened to a presentation by the hugely successful international retail jeweler, Michael Hill of Michael Hill Jewelers. He was addressing an audience of specialist retailers and made a very prophetic comment,

> *"It doesn't matter if you are an expert jeweler, an expert on cell phones or an expert on paint. The only thing that matters is being an expert on filling your shop with customers!"*

As Michael says, while you may have an expertise, the only thing that really matters is your ability to communicate the (perceived) expertise to your potential customers and develop lasting relationships with them.

The 80/20 rule of customer count

You may have a customer count of 100 per day. Assuming six day trading, that does not mean 600 unique people per week or 2,400 different people each month. Among the 2,400 will be 400 or so that come back over and over again. The 80/20 rule is alive and well in every known retail business.

If you have a cafe, the same 20 people may call in for a coffee each day at 10am. If you have a book shop, the same few people will call in daily or certainly weekly to browse the magazines, buy stamps, or the latest book from their favourite author. If you have a clothing shop, the same woman that bought the dress last month will be the one that buys the new season skirt this week.

One store tracked their top customers and found that the best customer spent $18,000 with them in one year! Number two customer spent $8,500 and number three spent $7,000. The top 100 accounted for a massive 80% of the store's entire turnover.

It is critical that you know your regular high spending customers. And not just who they are by name, but where they live, their cellphone number and their email. These 20% of your customers will be generating 80% of your turnover. Work out who they are and have a documented process for looking after them – or someone else will.

Local mass advertising is wasted unless...

...unless you are part of a national chain. This is explained as you read the next sections. If you are a single store trading under your own brand, then it is a waste of time.

Consider that you are a store operating from a single location in a city. Your options are to use mass media such as radio. But the area that would cover could be as much as a 100 miles radius. Are your potential customers really going to come from that far away? Of course not. No one is going to drive past 6 or 7 of the same type of store to yours. 80% of your customers will be from a 5 mile radius or a 5 minute drive.

So it makes sense to confine any promotional activity to this area only. This will save you loads of money and with the right strategy you should be able to dominate that area to the extent that every resident in that area believes you to be the 'best' or 'expert' provider of that product range or service.

As your perceived expertise grows, you can enlarge the area you promote to, but start with a small highly defined area – the one that 80% of your business comes from.

National chains are different, but...

I must qualify this by saying that mass media can work for national chains. If there is a chain of stores all trading under the same brand, then mass media can be used to set the scene, explain brand values, discuss the competitive advantage of the chain or make a specific offer.

However this comes with a qualifier. It ONLY works if the local branch takes advantage of it. Locally, the store should run a supporting promotion such as letterbox, in-store reminder material or perhaps even have a spruiker outside the door.

TV or press is subliminal. No one deliberately allocates time to watch a set of TV commercials or read press advertising. It is picked up by the brain and stored, but rarely evokes a call to action. However, there is the "Hansel and Gretel Effect"

The Hansel and Gretel Effect

Just as Hansel and Gretel followed a trail of goodies to the witch's cottage, you must do the same. If the brand is on TV, locally you must add the next piece of the trail. This could be in the form of a letterbox drop for example. When potential customers see your store, the window should have a poster reflecting the advertising, then when they walk in, a display of the promoted items.

This works because the customer's brain recalls the TV advertising when it sees the poster, and the letterbox item and the display. The converse is that if you don't put the rest of the trail in place, the national advertising is completely wasted

Put dots on a map

Have a way of collecting names and addresses of customers. The easiest way to do this is to run a competition. Then take all the entries home and have your kids put dots on a map that represent where they live (this is too boring to do yourself).

Invariably the dots are most dense around your store and as the radius grows, the dots get thinner. The vast majority of smaller retailers get their customers from within a 5 to 8 kilometre radius of the store. So why would you do mass advertising?

The vet who put dots on a map

A city vet was using radio and press to attract new customers, but was not convinced that it was working. So she put dots on a map to mark the addresses of her customers (since she kept a database). She was surprised to learn that over 70% came from a single suburb and a further 20% from a neighboring suburb up a valley.

So she stopped her media advertising and started a letterbox dropped newsletter that was seasonal in its topics. For example the main headline read, "What to do with your pets while you are on your summer holiday" and "Issues cats face over winter" She also arranged to write a regular column in the local free newspaper. Customer numbers increased and existing customers used his services more often. This is because she was seen as the local expert.

Be the guru

This is the only way to get customers from a wide area, to generate substantial referral business and to build non-price-based loyalty. You must become the guru in your field. This means having the most knowledge and perceived expertise for the range of customer's problems.

It is easier to do this than you may realize. This is because few retailers understand how to do it, so you can stand out in the crowd fairly quickly. The first step is to gain an understanding of the customer's needs. You will read more about this later.

Sales promotions, competitions, scratch-n-win and other devices for getting them into your store

These definitely work. They may seem clichéd and overdone, but they work. People love something for nothing. Customers in an area will go out of their way to drop off a competition form to win an iPod or even just a $100 gift card. It's human nature to try to get something for free.

Top customer generating prizes are without doubt small electronic consumer items such as iPods, iPads, cameras, the Nintendo Wii and similar. Make sure you match the prize to your customer. If you have predominantly females ages 25 to 45, then pick a trendy consumer item that appeal to this market. If they are mainly men ages 40 to 60, the prize would be slightly different.

An important component of making them work is to have the staff prompt customers. They should say, "Did you see our competition in your letterbox? (or in the email we sent or advertising)" Many customers may have seen it but have forgotten and need to be reminded. Produce the entry form and have them fill it in. They will appreciate it and you will have another name and contact details for your database.

You can tie entries to a purchase to avoid customers just running in with the entry form. For example, they can only enter if they spend $15. Make it a low value to encourage more entries. And of course for good regular customers, don't annoy them by insisting on this. Let them enter for free, as it creates a lot of good will.

There are many variations on this. Service stations often offer the scratch-and-win style, with prizes as small as a can of Coke. The more likely they are to win, the more entries you will get, so lots of small prizes is better than a small number of big prizes.

And of course, don't forget to create a database from the names on the entry forms. If you do not have a dedicated database management program (called CRM) then just use Excel, remembering to separate every field i.e. separate columns for first name, last name, each line of the address, email, cellphone and landline.

Roll up, roll up... the profit generating excitement of a spruiker!

This is a very old idea from many centuries ago and still works incredibly well. We know of two retailers who achieved between 30% and 50% increases in store performance for the days the spruiker was used.

A spruiker is a person who holds a microphone and stands outside your shop extolling its virtues. He or she would be inviting passing pedestrians to try samples of products, to buy certain items at discounted prices, to enter competitions and other similar offers. They can create huge excitement and a big gain in traffic count for the time they are there, which is typically two days.

The big gain is from customers who may never have been into your store before. They will wander in out of curiosity and the strength of the deals on offer for the day. These only work however if the store is geared for the occasion. This means getting staff and key suppliers behind it to offer demonstrations, sampling and special deals.

Suppliers are generally quite willing to use this to launch new products and to also have their own staff on hand as experts. An experienced spruiker will know how to advise on the set up and brief the staff.

Your next customer is standing in front of you! Turning browsers into buyers

This is the fastest way to grow your customer count. They have already taken the time to park, walk to your store (possibly on the way to somewhere else) and have the time to stroll into your store. That's the expensive part taken care of. Turning them into buyers is achieved by your team understanding how to engage browsers in conversation. Here are a few ways to do this.

- Ask them if they would like to enter your competition to win a prize. They may not buy that day but now you know who they are and they can be added to your database.

- Start the conversation based on the item they are looking at. For example, (clothing shop) "what sort of shirt are you after?" or (book shop) "He is such a good author, have you read anything else by him?" or (kitchen ware) "Are you looking for something for yourself or for a gift for someone?"
- Compliment them on an item of clothing or something about them. This starts a conversation and allows you to then bring their attention to your latest offering or comfortably ask what they are after. Use this technique with caution as you don't want it to sound contrived. It must be sincere.

If a customer moves from 4 visits a year to 6, that's a 50% gain in customer count

Re-read the headline. Getting brand new customers is REALLY expensive as it could involve a better location, more promotional activity or other expensive techniques. But if they already buy from you, you must have a strategy for getting them back more often than they may have originally planned. This can be achieved through such devised as:

- Loyalty programmes or customer clubs
- Understanding their problems and offering future solutions as well as for the immediate one

- Inviting them back. Say, "I look forward to seeing you again. Let me know how you get on with this item"
- Being the 'expert' in your field so they won't want to go anywhere else. This is the biggie
- Use bag stuffers to introduce new or commentary products to the customer
- The total shopping experience is what counts. If they enjoyed it in all its various parts, then they will be back.

It's the TOTAL shopping experience that counts most

When a customer sees your shop for the first time, what do they see? A tidy, well presented inviting store? When they walk in the door are they greeted with a pleasant smile? Can they find what they are after quickly? Do they receive the advice they require to choose the right option for their specific problem? Is the actual purchase efficient and straight forward? Is the product they buy packaged well? Are they invited back in some way, such as invited to join a loyalty program?

It's the TOTAL experience that matters, which is made up of dozens of small components. And each one has to be identified, considered and constantly improved. Start making a list. An example list is shown here. Use this one or a modified version of it to brainstorm with your team on how to make small improvements in each area.

TOTAL Customer Experience Check List

FIRST SIGHT:
1. Outside signage: Is it clean and easy to read?
2. Outside lights: Do you look open? Are there lights blown?
3. Footpath: clean, uncluttered?
4. Carpark: clean, adequate?
5. Windows: single product display or cluttered?

THE WALK IN:
1. What do they see first upon entering? Is it appealing?

THE GREETING:
1. How are customers greeted?
2. Where are the staff normally standing?
3. What is the conversation starter?

THE SALES PROCESS:
1. Are customer's needs explored?
2. Did you devote enough time to the customer and not try to multi-task?
3. Do you feel you develop a rapport with the customer?
4. Did you ask them if they wanted to buy or just leave them hanging?

THE STORE LAYOUT:

1. Are specials and promoted products easy for customers to see and find?
2. Is the store cluttered? Easy to navigate around for all including push-chairs?
3. Are all displays and gondolas stacked no higher than shoulder height?
4. Are there dead spots?
5. Is there stock on the floor?
6. Are displays full and have computer generated price tickets? (never use felt pen)
7. Is the counter clear and uncluttered?
8. Are shelf price tickets easy to read?
9. Are categories clearly marked?

THE PURCHASE:
1. Was this made easy for the customer?
2. Do you accept all forms of payments with no fees?
3. Did you ask if they were a customer club member so they can get a discount or points?
4. Did you wrap the item if a gift?

THE FAREWELL:
1. Did you invite them to come back?
2. Did you invite them to join the loyalty program?
3. Did you say good-bye or wish them a pleasant day?

The power of bag-stuffers

These devices are so simple they don't deserve to work but they do. The idea is to put a small leaflet into the bag the customer takes away. It should be advice based or explain other elements to a collection. It should rarely be a price deal.

- **In a photographic store**, the leaflet should be about the problem the customer has. For example how to store the photos in such things as photo-books or to offer them as gifts by printing the photo on the side of a mug.

- **In a clothing or shoe store** it could be about how to care for the item or how to match colours in their wardrobe or latest trends.

- **In a hobby shop**, it could be tips on getting a better build result or 6 other models that make up a set to the one they bought.

- **In a book store** it could be a list of suggested summer reading for a specific age group or preferred genre.

Research says that they are definitely read by the customers, but only acted on if they are interesting and perceived as value to the reader. If they are advice or tips based, they reinforce your position as the guru in your industry.

Loyalty programs – worth it or wasted?

Definitely worth it! But while offering 10% off for being a club member or your fifth cup of coffee or photo print free is a nice gesture, it should be more substantial than that. You can see proof of how dis-loyal patrons can be when the cafe customers pull out 20 coffee cards to find the one for that cafe.

Loyalty clubs work if they are designed to develop truly loyal customer relationships. This comes from offering advice, tips, free stuff, collegial events (customer evenings) and making it fun. As a very rough guide, customer club communication should be 60% advice and tips, 20% soft sell and 20% hard sell. This is easy to manage, for every 10 messages, make sure 6 are advice, 2 are soft sell and just 2 are hard sell.

People are sick of specials and deals being thrust down their throats. They want to know how to improve their lives through the use of the product, which is why advice and soft sell are far more effective. Think of this as having a conversation with your customers and imparting your expert knowledge.

Advice and tips: (60%) this is how to use the product, case studies and advice on others things related to the products and services you offer in terms of how it fixes the customers problems.

The soft sell: (20%) Up and coming products or ranges, your staff member of the month, changes to the store,

The hard sell: (20%) special offers and deals.

Is Facebook a loyalty program?

Yes it is, as by definition it generates a conversation with your customers. Facebook can sometimes be used to grow your customer base, but its true effectiveness is in maintaining loyalty and growing sales per customer. This is because it is the perfect forum to prove your expertise and achieve 'guru' status in the minds of existing customers.

This book doesn't cover how to make Facebook work for your business, but there are literally thousands of articles and videos on the Internet that can give you guidance on this. Watch and read and learn.

An important point about a Facebook strategy for retail is that setting it up might be free and only take a few minutes, but you must post DAILY comments and have a strategy for growing the fan base of your page. These can be quite labor intensive. So make sure your methods are all worked out and in place well before launching your page.

Example customer contact plan for a sports shop:

January: A welcome to the New Year and advice on 5 ways to trim down after Christmas (Advice)

February: Offer a special on school sports items (Hard sell)

March: Tips on choosing sports shoes (Advice)

April: Article on why some tennis racquets cost $25 while others cost $400 (Advice)

May: Picture and profile of a staff member who is an expert in... (Soft sell)

June: 10 ways to avoid winter sports injuries (Advice)

July: 5 ideas for low cost indoor sports (Soft sell)

August: Fantastic end of season sell out deals (Hard sell)

September: Enter a competition to win $500 worth of equipment of your choice (Soft sell)

October: Tips on how to squeeze 15 minutes into your busy day for exercise (Advice)

November: Preparing for the Christmas break to avoid strains and sprains (Advice)

December: 7 essential items to take on holiday with you (Advice)

The loss leader

Use with caution, but it can sometimes be a good tactic to choose one product to use as a loss leader. Be careful that you have a clear strategy behind the loss leader, or customers may just come in for that heavily discounted product only. Your team must be well briefed on how to convert these bargain hunting buyers into a good value sale, or it is a waste of time.

Choosing the product is important. If you are a bookshop it can't be totally unrelated like soap powder. It must be something that is consistent with the type of store. Ask your suppliers for any lines they may be deleting to make way for newer versions or to change packaging. They may have a thousand units of an item that has no real value to them anymore.

It must have an exceptional price point to work. For example, you may sell a popular item for $15 that is about to be changed in some way. If you take the suppliers entire stock for say $1 each, you could offer it at 99 cents. Don't try to profit on the deal, the point here is its draw card value, not the profit it generates in itself. If you tried to sell it for say $5.99 you are completely missing the point and the impact will be lost.

You can qualify the purchase by tying it into other purchases. For example, if they spend $15 on any other purchases in the store, they can get this item for $1 instead of the $15 it may have been offered at before.

What 3 things is your competitor doing better than you?

If your nearby competitors appear to be getting good customer numbers, find out why. Send in spies. Get family members or your own staff to go and visit them like a secret shopper. Their mission is to report back on 3 things the competitor is doing better than your store.

This is a powerful way to improve your store's performance. Have your staff member or friends look at such things as merchandising ideas, how they were treated by staff, prices, store layout, cleanliness and 'feel' of the store.

This is not designed so you can become a me-too store and just copy your competitor. It's all about identifying strengths and weaknesses and then addressing them in your own way. This really works!

Give the school kid a clipboard

Hire a couple of 17 year old school kids to go around your store with a clipboard. Have them start in the parking area and then move into the store and list everything they see as not perfect. This could include rubbish, non-dusted shelves, poorly maintained displays, faded singage, blown lights, difficult to navigate areas, staff not being attentive, a cluttered counter, unpacked stock on the floor, confusing price tickets... the list goes on.

It will be amazing how many tiny faults they come up with. You and your team are simply blind to them as you work there every day. Tell them to be as picky as possible and fill the paper on the clipboard. Then go through the list and make it your objective to have them all done within a specified number of weeks. Then do it again six months later. It's the little things that mean the most to customers.

Becoming the guru

This is the key to making big money in retail. If you can become the guru in your field then you don't have to attract customers through discounting and patronage will grow through word-of-mouth. But in the competitive field you are probably in, how do you do this? Here are some ways that this can be achieved.

Dress like a guru
If you are a pharmacist, dress yourself and your staff in white like the medical professional you are. If you are in a menswear shop, dress your team in the best you have in store. If you have a sports shop, dress the team in sportswear. If you are a bicycle shop, dress in shirts that look like racing tops. These might all sound a bit clichéd but this works.

Act and talk like a guru

The way to do this is to understand the customer's needs and then provide informed answers. Nothing impresses a customer more than showing your expertise. Let me give you an example of the right way and the wrong way in a hobby shop.

The WRONG way:

Customer: "Hello, I see your radio control Spitfire there. Is it easy to assemble and fly?"

Staff: "Maybe half an hour to put together and another half hour to test and muck around. You would be flying in an hour."

Customer: "And what does it come with?"

Staff: "This one is just the aircraft. You will have to buy the radio transmitter separately. $299 for the plane and about $200 for the radio gear"

Customer: "Ok... and what level of experience is needed?"

Staff: "Well if you have flown any radio control aircraft before you would be fine"

Customer: "And are their other models in the range like a P51 Mustang or Corsair?"

Staff: "Yes, there are about six I think in the range. Here is a brochure on them"

Customer: "Thanks"

The customer then leaves the store reading the brochure. The customer is happy but the sale is lost and the store doesn't know who he was.

The RIGHT way:

Customer: "Hello, I see your radio control Spitfire there. Is it easy to assemble and fly?"

Staff: "Yes it is. Can I ask if you have built or flown radio control aircraft before?"

Customer: "No, I'm quite new to this"

Staff: "Well, let me take you through how you can get into this amazing hobby"

Customer: "That would be great"

Staff: "Well, I'll just go and get three aircraft for you, a beginner, a more advanced and the ultimate to build up to, so you can get a good idea of how to logically progress through the hobby"

The customer walks out having spent $400 on an aircraft and radio control gear. The staff member also invites him to an evening for budding hobby pilots, whereby he can become part of a community of like minded individuals that treat this shop as their "club house" He is asked for his contact details so the store can send him information about new models.

But most importantly, this customer now considers the staff member the GURU of radio control models and a long term loyal relationship has just been started.

Have 'guru tips' sheets

Have a set of sheets drawn up of the 10 most common questions or issues customer ask about. Have them each put in advice format on a single sheet of A4, A5 or even folded DLE size brochure.

If your name is Ken, than call them "Ken's tips on..." and include your photograph on them. Use them as bag stuffers and to give to enquiring customers.

Have a consulting room or table

When a customer asks about something, it is a good idea to have an area dedicated to consulting or demonstrating products. In the hobby shop example above, you could have a circular table on the floor where you put each model to show them.

In a sports shop, have a fitting area dedicated to fitting sports equipment like racquets, clubs and shoes. The customer feels special this way, as you have taken them to the "consulting area". All specialists have consulting areas, so why not you?

Call yourself a guru

If you say it to yourself often enough it sticks. On your name badges, rather than have "Retail Assistant" have something that includes the word expert. For example, in a menswear, have the badge read "Personal Image Expert". In a bookshop, have "Children's book expert" and so on.

Make your TEAM the heroes and not the product

This should apply to the whole team. When you go to your GP, they will refer you to various specialists depending on your condition. You pay the GP $30 and the specialist $180. Why? It's because of the perceived additional expertise. So why not use this same principle in your store. In a sports store, one staff members could be the "Racquet sports expert" and another "Field sports expert" and so on. The credibility in their advice will soar.

Have a local press or magazine column

Rather than waste of time advertising, what about running a column called "Bob's Health Tips" for a health shop, or "Stephanie's Reading Guide" for a book shop, or "Steve's Image Guide for Men". Get the idea? You would probably have the pay for the space just like any other advertising, but the reader impact would be many times that of advertising. And your "guru" status would climb very quickly.

Reduce the size of your pond

If you reduce the size of the pond you swim in, you can be the big fish a lot easier. This is achieved by describing yourself in terms of a niche.

For example, you are not just a photographic shop. Describe yourself as an expert in photographic gifts. If a bookshop you could be a magazine specialist. Make the pond smaller by redefining the market and you are almost instantly the expert.

Run a blog and Facebook page

Blogs are read, as are Facebook pages. It would take another volume to explain how to use these effectively, but they are not hard. They are free to use and can be incredibly effective.

Go to the internet and search for "How to make Facebook work for a retail store" and you will get thousands of examples and how-to videos.

The main thing to understand here is that these work! Standard web sites do not. The main reasons people buy anything online is convenience and price. Supermarkets use this effectively as it is convenient to shop from your home. Electronics are bought online because they are cheaper. So unless you have an exceptional deal to offer, go the blog way and build your perceived expertise. Don't use it to try to sell anything.

Chapter 4

Driving up the average spend per customer

The most important bit first

Growing the average spend is not only a good way to grow the gross profits as it doesn't require any new customers, but it is also an indicator of how much the customers treat you as the 'guru'.

The more they spend the more they value your advice, service and product offering. If one store of your kind averages $25 while another averages $45, it is worth spending time finding out why. While it could be partly due to the socio-economic area they trade in, it is far more likely to be the people in the team and the rapport they are able to build with the customers.

Retailing is selling

Retailing is selling, retailing is selling, retailing is selling. What part of this don't some of your team understand? It is amazing how many times we hear retail staff saying, "I work in retail, I would hate to be in sales" Huh? To be fair, if they prefer, they can see it as helping people by offering solutions to their problems. But the solutions must be comprehensive and result in the customer willingly parting with money.

What is your customer's problem?

Customers never buy products. They only ever buy a solution to a problem. This is extremely important for your team to understand. Once they get this in their minds, it is amazing how it alters the way they treat the customers.

The best possible strategy is to look after them and to understand their motives for buying. Ask questions. Here is an example conversation from a pharmacy.

Customer: "Hello, can I have a small packet of Panadol please?" (price $14)

Staff: "Sure, is it for you?"

Customer: "Yep, for me"

Staff: "Can I ask what sort of pain you have? Different pain killers work better on different pains"

Customer: "Oh... a headache actually, a nagging pain in the back of my head"

"Staff: "How long have you had that?"

Customer: "Started yesterday, then back this morning"

Staff: "Have you taken anything for it already?"

Customer: "Yes, some Lemsip, because I was worried it might be the start of a cold"

Staff: "Did you know that Lemsip contains paracetamol, the same active ingredient as Panadol. You could accidentally overdose."

Customer: "You're kidding! Can you really overdose on paracetamol?"

Staff: "Yes you can, are you taking any other medications?"

Customer: "Yes, diabetes tablets."

Staff: "That's ok, no conflict there, but what I would recommend is that you take Nurofen as it can complement the effect of the paracetamol in Lemsip. Can I also suggest that you increase the amount of Vitamin C with a high-potency supplment, as you could be right in thinking that it is the start of a cold."

The customer paid $57 for the items suggested and went out very happy indeed that the staff member had taken the time to truly understand his problem. He will definitely be back.

Understand the customer's problem

No one shops without a problem to solve. Do they need a gift? Do they need a new pair of shoes to keep up with fashion trends? Do they need a good book since they just finished their last one? Your job is to find out what the problem is. If you don't, then how can you offer them anything?

Consider these three scenarios in a shoe shop:

The WRONG way:

Staff: "Hi there, can I help you with anything?"

Customer: "No thanks, just looking"

The conversation is dead in the water and almost impossible to recover. Whether they buy or not is no longer under your control.

Another WRONG way:

Staff: "Hello, are you after any particular type of shoe?"

Customer: "Um... yeah, something a bit casual"

Staff: "Well we have a great special on these ones right now. What do you think?"

Customer: "Mmmm... they are nice, but not sure. Might just keep looking around the store"

Staff: "Sure, if you need any help, just ask and feel free to try any of them on"

Conversation halted. Once again, whether they buy or not is no longer under your control and they may walk out. And you offered the special item first – NEVER offer a price deal first.

The RIGHT way:

Staff: "Hi there. I see you are looking at a casual shoe. What would you be wearing it with?" (The staff member is identifying the customer's 'problem')

Customer: "Oh hi, umm... well jeans mostly"

Staff: "Would you be wearing it with anything else?"

Customer: "Umm... yes... I also have some black three-quarter pants that I would want to wear it with"

Staff: "Well just about anything goes with jeans, but let's discuss the three quarter pants. Can you pull the legs of the jeans up a few inches? Then you can see what the shoes would look like"

Customer: "Good idea" (she does that)

Staff: "Let me get you three different popular types and see which one you think you would like best with those kinds of pants"

See the difference? You totally control the sale, by first determining the customer's needs and then offering a range of solutions. The customer will see you as a friend and not a salesperson. The chances of a sale are almost 100% and they may even buy two or three pairs if you explore the colored tops they may wear those pants with.

The lesson here is that you must first identify the problem, being the reason they want to buy. In the pharmacy example, the customer didn't want the branded pain killer Panadol, he wanted his nagging headache fixed. In the shoe store example, the customer had a need for shoes to go with two different types of trousers. Brainstorm with your team on good opening lines and questions to ask to identify their problem.

Clothing or shoes – "What will you be wearing it with?"
Gift shop – "Who is it for?"
Camera shop – "What sort of photos would you be taking?"
Electronics shop – "What brand have you had before?"
Pharmacy – "What have you found worked best for you?"
Sports shop – "How often do you play?"
These questions are designed to have the customer tell you more about what they are buying it for. This is identifying their problem and as a result you can tailor a solution for them. They will see you as far more than a retailer this way – they will see you as the expert or guru in your field. This is the real secret to growing a retail business. More on this in the next chapter.

Your recommendations are far more powerful than you realize

Customers rarely come in to buy a specific item. They want advice on the best one for the problem they have. Few will say that, but it's implied. If a customer comes in and says,

"Do you have X brand?" then the wrong initial response is to say, "No but we can get it in for you". The best first response is, "Can I ask what you are going to use it for?" then once they reply, you can say, "Actually we have found this brand Y to be more popular/better for that."

You have considerable power in ability to recommend. Customers expect you to know which the best one is as they assume you wouldn't be working there if you didn't. It is false thinking to take the customer's request literally and try to satisfy their exact request. It is simply their opening sentence, as they may not know about alternatives.

You have immense power in your suggestions and all you have to do to appreciate their problem to be able to make use of your power.

The sub-formula for customer spend

The average customer spend is the average stock item price multiplied by the items per customer. So for example, if you average 1.5 items per sale with an average item value of $20, then your average customer spend will be $30.

If you can move the average items per sale to 1.8, but maintain the $20 item average, then the average spend becomes $36. Equally, if you move the item average to $24, but maintain the 1.5 items per sale, that also becomes an average customer spend of $36. So to build the average customer spend, you should look at both these factors.

Building item price

It is often easier to build the item price, but this depends on the type of store you have. The easiest way to do this is to always offer the largest size first. If you have three sizes of an item, say $20, $30 and $40, then offer the $40 one first. The pitch can be built around the greater value for money or how they won't run out or whatever is appropriate.

People will seldom if ever say, "That's too small, I would rather have the bigger more expensive one" so do not shop UP! But if they say, "That's a bit big, do you have a smaller size?" This is fine, but if you don't offer the larger one first they will not even consider it. So make it a store policy to always reach for the biggest or more expensive one first.

Items per customer

This primarily comes from understanding and addressing the customer's problem.

Companion selling, or how no single product will fix the problem

"Do you want fries with that?" is the first thing most think of when companion selling is mentioned. But while that famous line has done well for McDonalds, that's the wrong way to think about companion selling. It's better to think about it as being how no one product will do the job.

Go back to finding out the customer's problem. If they buy a shirt, their problem is to give themselves a better wardrobe. So if the shirt is shown to the customer with a pair of trousers or skirt, then they may decide to buy the combination. If they come in to buy a book, direct them to other books by the same author. Companion selling is about understanding the problem and offering a more complete solution.

It works when the offer is related to the original item. For example, if they want a model airplane, ask if they have the right paints. If they buy a lipstick, ask if they have lip-liner. If they want paint, offer them brushes or a roller. If they buy a computer, offer them a back-up hard-drive. Everything will have a natural companion item.

The way to start this is to identify the top 10 sellers in your store. Then have the staff brainstorm on what other products naturally go with each one. This list then gets tapped to the counter or memorized by staff so that it becomes automatic to ask. Once this has been successful, add a new list of 10. You can incentivize the staff by offering a prize to the most companion sales in a week.

Closing the sale

Few customers say, "Ok, I'll take that" Instead they expect you to do that for them. Many sales are lost because the sales staff say, "Well I'll be over there if you need more help" or "I'll leave it with you to decide" You may think you are taking the pressure off them and doing them a favor, but you must remember that they came in for your advice on which one to buy. If they didn't they could have bought the item at a discount store or on the internet.

There are two easy ways to close the sale and get the buyer to commit. The first is to assume the sale and say, "Can I take it to the counter for you?" or a variation might be, "Can I ring it up for you?" or "Let me wrap it for you".

The other way is to offer alternatives. Examples are, "Which size did you want?" and "Would you want the blue one or the red one?" or "Did you just want a single bottle or the special deal on three?"

You can also phrase this in terms of payment, such as, "Will you be paying with EFTPOS or credit card?" or as a question, "How will you be paying for that?" In all cases, if they don't want to buy they will tell you, but unless you ask, the sale can often be lost.

Chapter 5

The psychology of pricing and its impact on sales

99c, 50% off, 2for or Save $20 or a Bogo?

Confused? So are your customers if you get the pricing structure wrong. Let's say you have a $29.99 item. How do you discount the price to maximise its attractiveness to customers? This could be worded as any one of:

- Buy one, get one free (known as a 'Bogo' or a 'Bogof')
- Only $15, save $14.99
- 50% off
- 2 for $29.99

They all say the same thing, so which one works best? In one instance, it was a man's shirt and the simple $15 moved the most stock. In another instance, it was a bottle of vitamins and the 'Buy one, get one free' worked best. In a third example, novels in a bookstore, the '2 for $29.99' worked best. The only way to really know is to test it. However there are some guidelines that may help.

Consider the frequency of use

If the product is one that is used on an ongoing basis by customers, for example vitamins, then allowing them to buy multiples at a discounted price works best. So a 'buy-one-get-one-free' or '2 for...' or even '3 for...' can work well. If it is a product where a second one seems redundant, for example a toaster, then this would never work. But a 50% off or Half price would certainly attract buyers.

Its perception, not reality that counts

When you see a car going for $19,999, that's really $20,000, but incredibly most people read it as $19,000. Our brains don't process the '999', which is why so many retailers take advantage of this setting their prices to end with a 99c. It has been researched that setting the 99c at the end of the price also leads consumers to believe they got a bargain.

Interestingly, a recent study showed that when shopping in a store, by catalogue or by website, people are likely to spend more when they see high prices around them, on items completely unrelated to what they want to buy. This is apparently due to being slightly conditioned to the higher prices by association.

Price points

It is far better to price an item at $49.95 than at $50. If you work on standard mark-ups, say 50%, then it may be that the price works out to be $31.20. This is a ridiculous price, but it's surprising how often we see it. When it comes to the dollars, try to keep it just under the nearest $10 mark. So in that case of $31.20, you will sell far more at $29.95 even though you will be slightly lowering your gross margin.

Strangely, if you have an item for say $36, putting it up to $39.95 can actually increase sales. This is because we are so programmed to think in terms of prices just under the $10 point. When it comes to the cents, either set your system to price everything at 49 cents or 95 cents or 99 cents. These are the three that are proven to get the best response.

The influence of urgency

If you put a single item on the counter under the banner "One Day Sale" it will see well. People don't like the idea of missing out. Flash sales are becoming quite the rage. J.C. Penney ran "7 hour steals", offering cotton bath towels for $3.69, reduced from $7.99, and 70% off gold and sterling silver jewellery. Its due to a sense of exclusivity. Taking it one step further, one department store ran hourly specials –

announced on the store's internal public address system. Select items were up to half price, but only for that hour. You could see the customers gravitate to the relevant department as each special was announced.

Price to fit the situation context

It's all to do with context. If a fridge is a bit over $2,000 normally but being offered at $1,100, how you promote it? You could say "Now, just $1,100" or perhaps "45% off" or maybe "Save over $900!!" In this instance, the last one worked best as saving $900 on anything is a lot.

The reason it worked best is that you don't buy a fridge every day so don't really know the price. So 45% off is a good offer, but what is that in dollars? Just $1,100 is also a good offer, but how good – since you don't buy one very often, (probably only one every 10 years) you have no context for that offer. But saving a whopping $900 sounds so much!

You must get inside the heads of your customers and understand how they would think. What would make the most sense to them? You will have heard the old analogy about petrol. If I offered you a gallon of petrol for your car at $10 a gallon, you would turn it down, saying it is way too dear. But if you were desperate to get home and that was the only gas station on your way, you would moan about it, but you would pay it. Price is so much based on context.

Don't tell me what, tell me why

Give me a reason to buy and I will ignore the price. I saw a 3-tier wooden stand in a shop recently. I had no idea what it was for. It had a price tag saying $110. A shop assistant came up to me and asked if I needed help. I asked her what this item was for. She said she didn't really know, but it would have "dozens of uses." Wrong answer!

Another customer overheard this and said, "Sorry to jump in here, but I have one like that. It's in my bathroom and I stack towels in the bottom two and face clothes in the top basket" Now I was intrigued. This made a lot of sense and I seriously considered purchasing it.

Don't tell me WHAT I can buy off you; tell me WHY I would want to buy it! Price moves down the leader of reasons to buy once you do this.

The presentation creates value for money

A farmer puts various fruit and vegetables items on display in a weekly Farmer's Market. He puts them on planks stacked on bricks as supports. He wraps them in brown paper and has hand-written price tickets. He gets DOUBLE what he gets from other sources of custom. Why? Because there is a perception that you are buying direct and no cost has been added for packaging. Yet you are paying more!

Words that can overcome a discount

"Limited time" entered our vocabulary as a result of McDonalds and now retailers of all types use it to good effect. You can generally put a premium on the price using this term. Other words that alter our perception of price are "Best value" as it means what it says. This should only be used for larger pack sizes. "Manager's Special/Pick" can work for special items. It doesn't even have to be discounted, it's like an endorsement.

Some stores do well when the sign includes "As seen on TV". This is because it implies a recognised popular brand and promotes recall. Once again it is not necessary to discount. "Please ask before bringing this to the counter" implies exclusivity or a special significance. "Imported" should be used with caution. In some cases it means cheap and nasty stuff (like clothing) and in others it means a premium product (like wine). "Limit 4 per customer" almost always means that customers will buy four (or whatever the number you used is). Depending on the product you may have to offer a discount with this as well.

"Cash back" offers are when you redeem a coupon for some element of cash back. This is used a lot on electrical goods such as computers. The main

What if someone down the road sells the same thing cheaper?

You may have a vitamin bottle containing 25 capsules that sells for $24.95. But the supermarket has the same item for $17.95. However the way to overcome this is to promote a different pack size, one that is far better value for money. For example, if they also make a container that holds 200 capsules, then promote that at say $59.95.

That way you can rightfully say that each capsule only costs 30 cents, compared to the supermarket price of 72 cents per capsule! This way you actually win on price as you are able to take the focus away from the price of the bottle.

Another way is to offer a gift-with purchase. This way you get a perceived price advantage by offering a high value item alongside it for FREE (a magic word) For example, you may have a fridge for $1,700 that is being sold elsewhere for $1,500. But if you offer a "FREE" microwave oven valued at $300, then you are offering more than $100 more value. The microwave won't cost you #300 of course; you may be able to get it for $100. Don't go head to head on price. Find a way to offer a "value" version of the product.

Recommend Retail Price (RRP)

What is the 'Recommended Retail Price' of an item? There is really no such thing, but various categories have products have an accepted industry mark-up. Gifts may have 150% and cosmetics 60% and so on. It can be a good idea to say "RRP $69, our price $49" however it only works if others in your field regularly price their wares at the RRP. A more successful and safer alternative is "elsewhere up to $69". But as a note of caution, it MUST BE $69 in the near vicinity otherwise you could be breaching fair trading laws.

As an extension to this, when you run a special, you must be careful not to make false claims. For example, let's say you normally retail an item for $40, but you know others sell it for $50. You cannot then offer it on special for $25 ($24.95 would be better) and claim "now 50% off" based on the full retail of $50 because you have never offered it for that price. You will have to say "Save $15" or "37% off" or "now only $25" or perhaps "elsewhere up to $50".

Chapter 6
How store layout can significantly affect store performance

Are you sending ransom notes?

You will have seen many films and TV shows where the kidnapper sends a ransom note made up of various letters cut out of other publications. This is what many stores accidentally do when it comes to image and design.

Take pictures of the outside and inside of your store. Then lay everything out on a table that a customer is likely to see from you. The pictures, labels, customer bags, newsletters, staff uniforms, a screen shot of your web site and any brochures and advertising. Do they all look the same, have the same colours, design elements and look like they were all designed on the same day by the same person? If not, you are sending mixed messages.

Look at them critically. Do they all use the same typeface, the same colours; is the logo in exactly the same place on every item? If anything looks out of place, the colours don't match or anything else is mis-matched, then you have an issue.

Take them all to a graphic artist and either have them re-designed or at the very least, replace the bad ones so they look like the good ones. Then just print each one as your budget allows or as they run out, so this way they are all eventually going to be exactly the same. This is an important part of building a brand.

It's worth having a new look at your visual image even if you don't change the brand. It will be a lot less expensive than you may think to do a makeover and psychologically it's a great way to start a new year and gives the store and team a boost.

Your nephew may be good, but...

Never ever, ever design your logo yourself, or get your 14 year-old nephew to do it! Why? Because you can tell. It is false economy trying to save money on the design elements. Design is an important element of your brand and can make a huge difference to how clients perceive you. In relative terms this is not expensive and should pay for itself almost immediately.

Cleanliness sells

A survey was conducted among the passengers on an airline. They were asked if their food trays were dirty, would they assume that the airline also does poor maintenance on its engines? The answer was a resounding "YES" from the vast majority. The strange logic that the passengers used was that if little things like the food trays were not cared for, then nothing else in the airline got much attention either!

So this leads to how your customers see your store. While you might know that you are offering outstanding expertise in your field, the customer is just as concerned about the little things like dust on the stock, an untidy cluttered counter and gaps on the shelves.

Understand flow through the store

Watch your customers. Where do they walk? Where do they not walk? Do you have what look to be dead spots? When customers first walk in are their eyes fixed on the counter, thereby not noticing the displays?

How you layout your store should be based on shopping patterns, ease of finding things and maximising exposure of your stock to those who come in. While layouts have to be slightly different for each type of retail, all stores have some common layout principles that must be adhered to.

Avoid runways

Many stores create a clear pathway down the centre of their stores for customers to get direst access to the counter at the back – BIG mistake! Some make it worse by changing the flooring down the runway to a different colored carpet or wood. This encourages customers not to look around and appreciate what else you offer. It makes dead spots even worse and the value of the sale low as they focus on the one item they came in for.

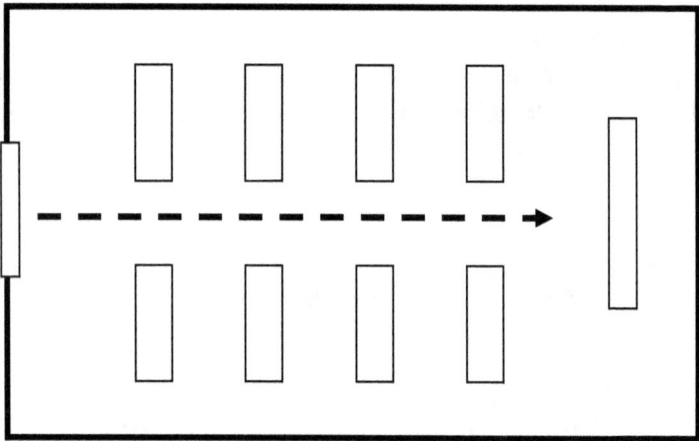

This is not to say that you should create a maze to wind through. That annoys customers and gives the impression of clutter. It must be clean and easy to navigate around and most importantly easy to find the various categories. You can still have a clear path down the middle, but it must be such that it encourages customers to look and venture left and right.

Good general layouts

This is a generalized layout but illustrates some key principles that would apply to every shop.

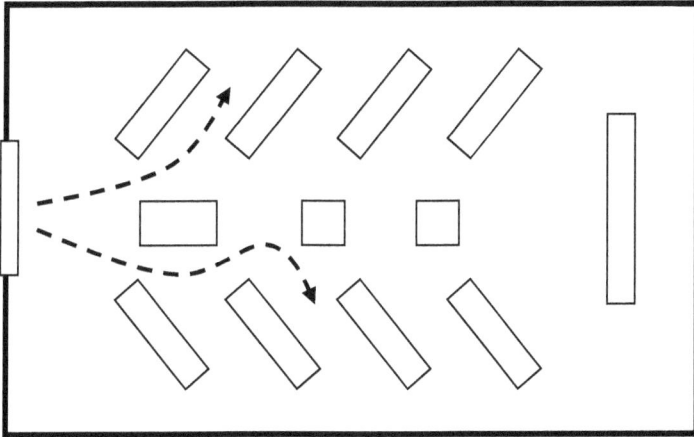

Make paths of travel such that they see it all
Make customers naturally want to wander between the gondolas and around interesting feature displays in their path.

Key stock on the walls, impulse stock on gondolas
Your core stock range should be on the walls. This gives more space to display it and allows for individual stock items to be highlighted. It also takes the customers out of the centre of the store where they could cause traffic jams and makes any conversations with them more private.

Put impulse and new lines on the gondolas and make sure these change frequently to give the impression that you always have new exciting stuff. It could be old stuff re-merchandised but it's the fact that it changes that is the most important.

Expose as much of the stock as possible

Putting gondolas on an angle or end towards the door is best. They don't block the stock on the walls this way. This configuration makes the store look bigger, brighter and less cluttered. It also allows you to use the ends for high-impact displays of single featured products.

Have dedicated feature areas

These can be sections of shelving (indicated by darker squares on the diagram) or specially made racks or bins (the dark squares). They break the look of long runs of merchandise, make key stock easier to find and highlight specific lines. Such products can be new, discounted or seasonal and not discounted at all.

"Spot X"

This is the place many shoppers pause for a second or two to get their bearings before venturing any further into the store. The location of the actual spot will vary for each store but is generally between one and one and a half metres inside the door. It is a very good idea to greet the customers when they reach this point so they feel welcome and are more likely to come in.

Gondolas – they can hurt as much as they can enhance your sales

The rule for height is shoulder height of a normal sized person. The highest piece of merchandise should be no higher than the shoulder so that the customer can still see everything in the shop. Not only is this a way to encourage browsing but it makes the shop feel bigger.

Avoid using supplier's stands. They are irregular in shape, never match anything else and you can only put one supplier's stock on them. Sometimes you can't avoid them due to the type of stock, but use them sparingly and only if you genuinely believe it will enhance sales.

One of the most productive things you can ever do is to simply de-clutter. Get rid of all stock on the floor, reduce the height of stock on gondolas and reduce the number of gondolas to the bare minimum. It is amazing how much of a difference this makes.

How to fix dead spots

Dead spots are quite often in the front corners. They can be anywhere depending on the type of store, but must be identified and fixed. You are paying your rent by the square metre so every square metre counts. A quick and easy fix is to identify a product range you have that is regularly asked for or not so responsive to impulse and put that in the dead spot. In pharmacies photo kiosks are often placed in dead spots to make that area productive.

The better solution is to look at the full layout of the store and redesign it to take the dead spots out. Have a shop designer come and consult on the layout. These people are nowhere near as expensive as you might imagine. Have them determine foot traffic flow through the store and come up with a new layout.

Most of the time this does not involve new fittings, just a rearrangement of existing fittings, a coat of paint, better lighting and fewer gondolas.

Lighting

This can make a surprising difference. Poorly lit areas of the store and an overall dull look can put shoppers off and cause dead spots. The brighter the store the newer and more appealing it looks to customers.

Have a lighting consultant come and see your store. Most lighting retailers can recommend someone for you. They can advise on brightening up the shop, the use of flood and spot lights to highlight specific areas and how to avoid lights casting shadows on stock and from customers.

If you have fluorescent lights, these gradually wear out and the light dims. Replace them regularly. Any blown lights should be replaced immediately as it looks to customers like you don't care. This includes lit stock cabinets and outside lights. Don't forget outside lights. Drive by your store at night and see if any are out.

Finding categories

You may know where everything is but your customers need to be able to work it out quickly as well. While the separation of some categories of product may be obvious, many are not. This is particularly a problem when you have long run shelving down one wall and the category distinctions are not that obvious. It is vital to the customer experience that you make it easy for them to find what they are after.

Separate categories with a display or promotional area. This can be as narrow or as wide as you wish; perhaps 600mm is a good size as that is a standard shelving size. Feature a single product from one of the two adjacent categories.

Have clear signage on the pelmets or other prominent places. You may think this is stating the obvious, but when a customer walks in for the first time, they scan the shop and need to find what they are after.

Make the top selling brands in each category the most obvious. Give them the eye level shelves and large numbers of facings. Customers recognize brands so if they spot the top brands they will know where to look, regardless of which ones they end up buying.

Never put stock on the floor

Be it in baskets, small bins or directly on the floor, this gives a trashy appearance. Don't do it!

Dump bins

These are a powerful way to increase sales of a particular product and give the impression of competitive pricing for the store. The natural reaction to a dump bin is that whatever is in it must be on special. So it doesn't matter if the product is at normal full price, it will still get a sales boost.

They are a good ways to stimulate sales of a slow moving product and introduce new products to customers. But do not waste the very valuable sales real estate they take up with junk products. All too often they are treated as clearing bins and are filled with expiring and discontinued lines, or cheap $5 items.

Only put high value high profit lines in them, for example nothing under $20. If you sell 8 a day at $20 (or preferably $19,99), making say $8 profit, that's $64. If the item is $5 and due to discounting only has a $1 profit, you would have to sell 64 of them to make the same money – which is very unlikely to happen.

Put them in high traffic flow positions. Near a counter, just inside the door and in the path most travelled in the store are best. DO NOT put them on the footpath or outside your entrance. It looks very tacky and makes your store look like a junk shop.

Have the sign above the dump bin explain what the product is and why it is important to the customer. Just the product name and price is not enough. It must be a motivating headline that clearly states the benefits to the customer. Ask yourself 'why would I buy this?' and the answer becomes your headline. Don't worry about how many words either, as long headlines have been proven to outperform short ones.

TV advertised product in-store

If a product you stock is advertised on TV, then build a display or put an "AS SEEN ON TV" ticket on it. This will trigger a memory in the customer's minds and make the sale far more likely.

Don't clutter the counter!!!

This is the single most important selling space in your store and many retailers fill it with stupid little items under $5. The principle many work on it that of supermarkets whereby the small chocolate bars are a final enticing impulse purchase after the main shopping effort.

But smaller retail shopping doesn't always work this way. The best use of counter space is two high value products only. This is the best place to introduce customers to new products. Exactly the same calculation works here as for dump bins. If you only sell three items a day from the counter make them worthwhile. And change the products regularly, either fortnightly or monthly.

Encouraging self-selection – making your shelves talk to customers

A product rarely speaks for itself. It needs something to explain itself to customers. Make up shelf strips that state the benefits. These can be printed onto coloured paper and slipped into plastic shelf strips. STATE THE OBVIOUS! No matter how obvious you think your description may be, that's what you write because customers forget.

Think how a customer would think. Do not put it in terms of product features, but rather in terms of benefits or why they would buy it. If its photo frames, do not write "Frames for all occasions" because there are too many occasions for the customer to appreciate any one of them. Instead write, "Give Grandma a framed photo of her new grandchild" If its gift lines, the strips could read, "Got her anything for Mother's Day yet?" If its books, it could be an endorsement such as, "Staff member Sally recommends..."

Chapter 7
Category and stock management

Category management

Treat each category in the store as a mini-project in themselves. Pick a category and then follow this process:

STEP ONE: Print out a category sales analysis from your Point of Sale System. List the products in each category in order from top seller to worst seller. Generate the report so that it includes percentage sales. If the system can't, then transfer the statistics to a spreadsheet and work out the percentages.

This gives you a quick snapshot of your stock and the performance of stock within each category. Of note is that if you do this regularly you will see changes. Some are seasonal and some are trends within your specific type of store.

Now before we go to the next steps, read the section on the next page regarding jams.

There were just too many jams!

US Professors Iyengar and Lepper tested consumer choice using jam. While out grocery shopping, consumers encountered a tasting booth which displayed either a limited (6), or an extensive (24) selection of different flavors of jam. The aim was to examine whether the number of options on offer affected consumer's subsequent purchasing behaviour. Consumers were allowed to taste as many jams as they wished.

The results: Nearly 30% of the consumers in the limited-choice condition subsequently purchased a jar of jam. By contrast, only 3% of the consumers in the extensive-choice situation purchased a jar of jam. Thus, consumers initially exposed to limited-choices proved considerably more likely to purchase the product than consumers who had initially encountered a much larger set of options.

This study was reinforced by psychologist Alexander Chernev, PhD, of Northwestern University. Chernev found that when people were offered variants of the same brand of toothpaste, e.g. cavity prevention, tartar-control and teeth-whitening types, they tended to switch to another brand that offered a single option.

It's too confusing, so reduce the choices

A big range is not a good idea. Not only does it consume your capital in stock, it confuses customers. So many retailers tell us that their competitive advantage is their range. With very few exceptions, that's nonsense. The 80/20 Rule is alive and well in every category.

A particular 'big-box' retailer normally has over 40 models of laptop computers on display. They train their staff to ask two leading questions when they see a customer looking. First, "What will you mostly be using it for?" and the other being, "Do you have a brand preference?" They then pick THREE models to show the customer.

This is a critical piece of the sale process. They are trained never to identify more than three to offer. Then further searching questions follow and the customer deliberates on which of the three they want. Only a handful of customers ever ask to see more than the three chosen by the retail assistant. They basically trust the three to be the most suitable to choose from based on how they answered the questions.

This is proven time and time again. when a jeweler shows the customer a big group of rings to choose from, the chances of a sale are significantly reduced as it is simply too confusing.

80/20 rule of stock display

Continuing with our category analysis,

STEP TWO: Add up the sales percentages so you have a cumulative tally. Invariably 80% of your sales will be coming from 20% of the stock. So let's assume that your sales print out for a particular category looks like this.

Category D

Item	Sales $	% of sales	Cummulative
A	$8,543	32.27%	32.27%
B	$5,378	20.32%	52.59%
C	$4,567	17.25%	69.84%
D	$2,890	10.92%	80.76%
E	$1,287	4.86%	85.62%
F	$934	3.53%	89.15%
G	$734	2.77%	91.92%
H	$644	2.43%	94.35%
I	$623	2.35%	96.71%
J	$489	1.85%	98.55%
K	$267	1.01%	99.56%
L	$47	0.18%	99.74%
M	$25	0.09%	99.83%
N	$23	0.09%	99.92%
O	$21	0.08%	100.00%
P	$0	0.00%	100.00%
TOTAL	$26,472		

In this example (very typical of many stores), items A, B, C and D make up 80% of the sales. All the rest only constitute 20% of the sales yet probably occupy at least half of the shelf space.

STEP THREE: Identify the waste of time items. In this case items K to P collectively account for less than half of one percent of the sales. These should all be deleted without argument. They are dead money, as taking up valuable space on shelves and the longer they sit there, the worse the impression it gives to customers.

STEP FOUR: Critically look at the items from E to J. Delete any that are no longer made, are near their expiry date or are falling in sales.

THE OUTCOME: Perhaps this exercise will reduce the total range in the category to just those from A to H. This is a very positive outcome. Now read about Mrs Smith.

What if Mrs Smith only buys THAT one?

The most frequent objection we get to reducing the range within a category is, "But Item L is the one Mrs Smith buys. We might lose her as a customer if we delete that line" There are two answers to this.

First, Mrs Smith is highly likely to be buying it simply out of habit and has never been offered an alternative. If you were to offer her an alternative, she will probably be very appreciative that you took the time to do that for her. Second, if that's all that Mrs Smith every buys, does it really matter if you lost her as a customer? The chances are that you won't lose her anyway. She has probably chosen to patronize your store due to its convenient location or easy parking and not for that item only.

% sales = % shelf allocation

STEP FIVE: Rearrange the shelves based on sales levels. If item A is 30% of your sales, then it should have 30% of the shelf facings for the category. Arranging them exactly to match their percentage in sales is not always possible, but is a guide.

In the example shown here, the BEFORE shelving is nice and tidy but in no way reflects the sales levels. The AFTER shelving shows huge number of facings for the top sellers and the bottom sellers no longer there. Customers love this approach as it is so easy for them to find the main brands.

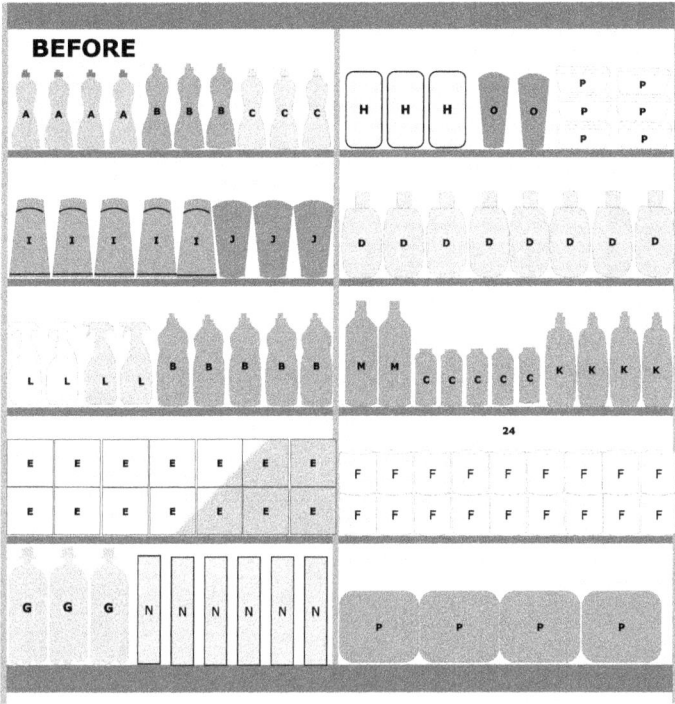

Initial reaction may be that Items A,B and C have far too much space, but this is a reflection of the relative sales levels. (Keep in mind that it may be an item with four flavors, or three variations) You will also note that the slower sellers have gone completely. As a result of rearranging the merchandise like this, you will find that sales of the top three go up even more and customers are less confused.

As a bonus, because you will be buying more of Items A,B and C, you can always achieve maximum discount so your gross margin will rise as well.

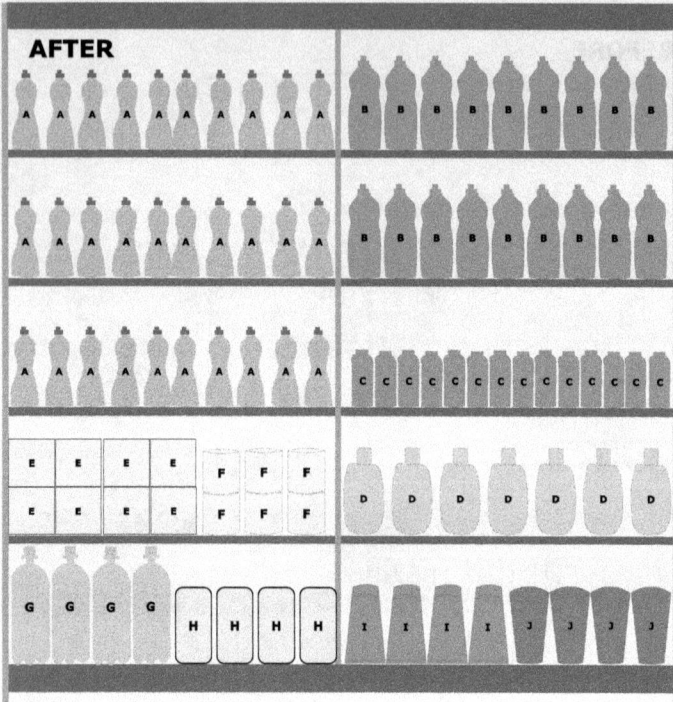

Dumping dead stock

Do NOT have fire sales with untidy cluttered sales tables.
They can severely damage the reputation of the store.
There are more effective ways to dump slow or dead stock.

1) **Counter bin One-Day-Sale** This is a highly successful
   way to move slow or dead stock. As in the picture, the
   idea is to make up a display box for the counter or a
   dump bin and call it "One Day Sale". Each day put a
   single item in it at a reasonably high discounted price,

perhaps cost price. It is dead anyway, so anything you get for it is bonus money.

You may have 10 of a dead item, so put all 10 in the box. If you sell 5 of them that day, that's 5 more than you would have sold of that line. Next day put a different item on the box and so on. This works because it focuses the customer's attention on that item which would otherwise be lost on the shelves.

2) **Hold a 'garage sale'** If you really want to do a clean out, make it a big one. Call it a 'garage sale' or similar and have garage sale signs all over the store, trestle tables and perhaps even dress your team in overalls. Make sure some good stuff is on special as well. It is highly likely that you can get supplier support for special deals.

3) **Ask the supplier to swap** You may be surprised how readily a supplier will swap old for new. Taking it back and crediting you is unlikely but swapping it for equal value new lines is in their interest as much as yours. It's worth asking. Some offer a standard 50% credit on old stock, so even this can make a big difference.

4) **Ask your wholesalers to swap** If you buy most of your stock through a wholesaler, you may be able to do a swap or get a credit as they have more sway with the suppliers.

5) Run a raffle

You may want to check the legal issues around this with your lawyer, as the regulations may vary depending on the state or country you trade in.

The idea is to pick a top selling item, say something worth $30, then put it in a gift basket with another $70 worth of slow or dead stock. The total value is then $100 and you can put it on your counter, offering 100 raffle tickets at $1 each. Don't offer 200 tickets as that is profiteering. You may even offer just 60 tickets at $1 to make it far more attractive to customers and the cost price may only have been $60 anyway.

6) Donate them to a community group

If you have a local group such as a play centre, mother's group or school sports team, make up the same gift basket and give it to them. Let them raffle it and your payback is being seen to be an active member of your community.

7) Throw them away

Dead stock is generally dead for a reason. Its either rubbish or quite simply no one wants it, or will ever want it. So in many cases you may have to just throw it away. It's taking up valuable shelf space and not helping the image of the store.

The power of shelf location

Moving a product up from knee level to eye level can have a dramatic effect on sales. Conversely, and equally dramatically, moving an item DOWN the shelving can hurt sales.

If you have an item that you believe deserves to sell better or is currently being advertised on TV, move it to eye level. If you have a slow item, before you throw it out completely, move it to eye level and you may move it faster without having to discount it or delete it.

The huge impact of shelf facings

A fascinating case study. A store stocked pregnancy kits and sales were slow. So the manager increased the shelf facings from two to seven and sales climbed by 220%!

This happened for the same reason sales increase as you move a product to eye level – it becomes much more visible. Experiment with various poor performing lines.

Some rules of display merchandising

The golden rule is KEEP IT SIMPLE. Single product displays will always out-perform multi-product displays. If you do not have enough product to fill a gondola end or display unit, ask the supplier for point-of-sale-material such as posters, large promotional product boxes or other items to fill the space. By way of example, you may have a gondola end with five shelves on it. You can cover the bottom three with a large poster and just have product on the top two.

Don't tell me what, tell me why – again!

Photo Frames **$24.95** Were $39.95 SAVE $15	**Stuck for a Xmas gift idea for Mother?** **Give her a framed photo of the grandkids** Photo Frames **$24.95** **SAVE $15**

These two example display tickets will have a dramatically different impact on sales. One simply tells the product and price, while the other offers the customer a reason to buy it. The discounted price should be a secondary reason.

Note that you may often be stating the obvious when writing the headline, but you need to do this or the product simply won't register in the mind of the browser.

The way to come up with a motivational headline is to ask yourself, "Why would someone buy this item?" and your answer becomes your headline. But don't forget to ask that question of someone from your target market.

Words that sell

Some words are known to be more powerful than others when it comes to selling. These should be used in displays and brochures and shelf talkers. While this list is clearly not exhaustive, these ones are proven to work

Big	Love
Safety	Health
Easy	New
You/Your	FREE
Save	Limited time
Only	One day sale
Best	Guaranteed
Value	Great buy

Examples of their use:
- Save **big** on this **value** pack
- **You** will **love** the feel of this on your skin
- **Free** gift with purchase
- **One day sale**
- **Best value** size
- Because we think **your health** is important

- **New** to our store
- **Easy** to use
- Buy 3 and **save**
- Buy one, get one **free**
- Only in store for a **limited time**
- **Saves you** time – **guaranteed**

Chapter 8

Improving the gross margin

The third factor in the formula

Maintaining a high margin is very hard when your competitors hold their prices at low levels. There are two ways to do this however that can make a big difference.

Buying at lower prices

Independent retailers often scratch their heads at this since they may not belong to a larger collective buying group. But there is more than one way to do this that does not require a buying group. Listed here are ways to improve your buy price, any or all of which may apply to you.

Be aware of your terms of trade

This one often surprises us. We are aware of one retailer who buys through a wholesaler who offers a 5% discount on 6 of any one item purchased and 10% on 12 of any one item. Yet he sends in orders for 3 or 4 of an item, or worse for 10! When questioned as to why, he said he had forgotten.

Another retailer offered a line at $29.95 and bought it for $21, so couldn't understand how the competitor down the road could offer it to customers for $19.95. They agonised over it for weeks until one day they asked the supplier, who told them that if they bought 100 of them, they could have a second 100 for free! This was a deal open to anyone.

This meant that the item came into store at $10.50, so even at $19.95, his gross margin was 47% compared to his previous offering at $29.95, which gave him a 30% gross margin. Be aware of your terms of trade!

Identify your top sellers

In earlier chapters we discussed looking closely at each category and only stocking top sellers (80/20 Rule). Arranging your shelves to represent sales levels gives top sellers even more exposure and greater sales.

This means that you can negotiate with suppliers to get greater discounts, merchandising support and often bonus discounts if you agree not to stock a competing brand.

Two buying styles

APPROACH #1:

"I'll order just 1 of each of the fifty items in this category. We need to keep stock levels down but we also want to offer a good range"

APPROACH #2:

"I'll order 20 of the top selling line, 10 each of the next two and 1 each of the next 17"

Buying style #1 – May sound logical, but it is flawed

- Constant out of stocks of top selling lines
- Customers unable to easily find the top brands
- Confusion due to the number of options
- 80% of the items will quickly become dead stock
- While the thinking is that this keeps the stock holding low, it hurts sales and means that no item is ever bought for the store at discounted prices

Buying style #2 – Counter-intuitive, but FAR better

- A reduction in individual items carried from 50 to 20 as a large range is almost meaningless to most customers

- Maximum discounts off wholesale on the top 3 as they account for 80% of sales in this category
- This way, out-of-stocks of high selling items will almost never happen
- Can increase the shelf facings of the top sellers dramatically. This invariably leads to increases in sales of that line and therefore the category (see section on "% sales = % shelf allocation")

Buy at promotion time for the future

Very often suppliers will run specials at say 30% off normal wholesale cost for one month to stimulate sales. You may normally sell 100 a month of this item. So you buy 200 and special them at a good price off retail and sales climb with margin maintained.

But the real opportunity is not the special period. It is AFTER the special has ended. You should buy 400 of that item at the 30% off wholesale, so that immediately after the special ends, you put the price back up to normal retail and your margin soars. Here is an example:

- Buy normally for $20, sell for $30 = 33% gross margin
  At $10 profit X 100 units per month, that is a $1,000 gross profit

- Buy at $14 (30% off wholesale), sell for $22 = 36% gross margin. At $8 profit X an increased 200 units due to the special, that's a $1,600 gross profit

- Now for the two months following the special, you have bought at $14, but return the retail price to $30. At $16 profit X 100 units (a normal month), that's $1,600 profit!

Sell at benchmark

Sell at benchmark for your area, never below. It is easy to find out the prices of key lines at your main competitor's stores. Have your staff phone them or wander in incognito.

There is no need to ever be cheaper for normal retail lines unless you are a dedicated discounter. If you are $14.95 and a competitor $27.95, that will not make one ounce of difference to sales levels, so you may as well match them.

Stores we have worked with have seen increases in gross margin by as much as 3% just by putting prices to benchmark for that item. 3% on a turnover of $750,000 is an extra $22,500 on your bottom line. That's a junior staff member paid for.

Chapter 9
Your team – the single most expensive yet profitable item

This topic is a book in itself

But despite this, we hope to cover some of the most critical elements when it comes to staff and their impact on your business. How they treat your customers makes a phenomenal difference.

Think about your own retail experiences. With some you come away feeling like you were an annoyance whereas with others it's like you made a new friend. This will very much dictate whether you go back there or not. In one case it was a clinical transaction, but with the other it was an emotional connection.

Many customers follow staff rather than the store. This is evidenced by the way customers follow "their" hairdressers and travel agents. We have also seen this in hobby shops, pharmacies and even service stations.

Treat staff like assets

Like all other business assets, staff need maintenance. If assets aren't looked after properly you often don't find out that they have sustained damage until there is a breakdown and even if this is reparable, it is never the same afterwards because there is always a scar.

Just like a new piece of machinery, they must be run-in, regularly maintained, looked after with care and even reconditioned if necessary. This chapter will give some pointers on how to do this.

8 ways to reduce the recruitment risk

1) Define the job and tasks clearly before you advertise. Know what you want done and then draw up a list of skills and attributes the person being recruited will need to have

2) Make sure you know what is a reasonable remuneration structure for the job and be willing to review it if necessary.

3) Draw up a shortlist of 2 to 3 applicants. Get a second opinion from another staff member or a respected outsider

4) Allow an hour for each interview and have a prepared interview form that you follow through with each

candidate. Make sure two of you conduct the interview so that you can compare notes.

5) Personality assessments and aptitude tests are helpful and very realistically priced and are another useful tool to find out more about the candidates.

6) Conduct at least TWO reference checks on the preferred candidate and make sure one is with a previous employer. Again, use a structured reference checking form. This is vital component of any recruitment process. Otherwise you are solely relying on what the candidate tells you.

7) Remember the adage 'recruit for attitude and train the skills'. Don't be hung up on the fact that they may not have worked in your particular field before.

8) Finally, have a good induction programme, which rapidly decreases the time to becoming effective.

You might be tempted to take shortcuts. Think about the risks and do so at your peril. Expect it to take time to find the right person and be prepared to devote a reasonable amount of your own time to finding them.

So they turn up for work, now what?

A true story. Sarah arrived enthusiastically at her first day in her new job. As arranged, she met with her boss and was greeted with "You're being paid good money, so I expect you to be able to get up to speed quickly." Training consisted of 'on-the-job' experience, watching other team members and getting what she could out of the reps that called. Six months down the track, Sarah was on six weeks stress leave due to her boss constantly being on her back about performance, was actively on the market for a new job and telling her story to anyone that would listen. Sarah left within 12 months of starting. The cost of the boss's behaviour was huge.

The answer to this was the simple concept of a staff induction program. Staff induction is the equivalent of setting up a machine for a factory. You don't expect a machine to run immediately without being properly calibrated to make sure it is running at optimum performance.

New staff induction program

The reason staff inductions don't usually happen is that many employers don't know how to run one. Below are a few tips to get you started.

- On the first day, simply tail another staff member to get a feel for the place. Do not let them serve customers, if approached their job is to find someone else. You might even like to give them a badge with the title "Trainee"

- Day two is to get them familiar with systems and processes. Spend time going through the routine housekeeping – processing sales, taking phone calls, opening and closing the store, processing stock when it comes in and so on.

- From then on, have a training process worked out. This is to include sales training, preferably through an outside agency and have contacted some supplier reps to arrange product training,

- Spend an hour at the end of each day reviewing the day and answering questions. Pay particular attention to where you believe further training may be required.

One of the key aspects to the induction programme is breaking down the learning into digestible chunks. Too often people get thrown in the deep end and have to find out things for themselves, or get too much information on the first day then forget most of it.

Sharing performance targets

A highly motivating factor can be sharing store performance targets. For example, you may currently do:

	NOW	TARGET	
Sales for the day:	$3,840	$4,000	
Sales per customer	$32	$33.33	
Items per customer:	$1.3	$1.3	(no change)
Customer numbers:	120	120	(no change)

The key improvement you are after is the value of each sale. When you set targets, make them modest increases and only change one variable at a time.

In the example, the sales for the day will rise if the sales value rises, so one target may be the result of another. Discuss these with staff and have them help you set them. Post the results on the staff notice board and have graphs if it helps.

How to DE-motivate your team

People are de-motivated by behaviour that they think is unfair or inappropriate. This includes things like inequitable pay rates This is particularly an issue as your team members get better at their jobs. You need to make sure that they get a fair share of bonuses, trips and other supplier benefits. Otherwise, you can expect good staff to leave. Not dealing with inappropriate behaviour from colleagues is a huge de-motivator. Another is perceived favoritism.

Laziness from the boss can be an issue. If the staff see the boss doing very little but arriving in the flash new car and taking overseas holidays, that causes resentment.

How to motivate your team

The opposite to these are conscious activities that do motivate the team. These include:

- A sense of achievement – Give them a task and then let them do it. Despite the odd mistake, they will have a sense of achievement that can be very rewarding.

- Recognition for effort – If they do it well, tell them

- Responsibility – being trusted to do the job. Do not breathe down their necks.

-	Being allowed to grow in the job – discuss their career aspirations and whether there are ways you can help

- Give them responsibility – Let them do some of the buying and do not interfere, despite your own thoughts that they are buying the wrong stuff. If they buy it, then it's their responsibility to make sure it sells.

Rewards other than money

Rewarding performance can come in a bunch of shapes and sizes, and money is not the only way. The reason for rewarding performance is to make the person feel valued so that they are motivated to stay and do a good job for you.

Find ways to surprise and delight your team. Don't make it a weekly event because the spontaneity is lost and then the purpose of surprising and delighting staff is lost. Things you might do to reward the team:

-   Morning tea or lunch shout
-   Organize a picnic so their families can be there.
-   A day off
-   Dinner and a show or just dinner
-   Gift baskets
-   Personalized gifts (selected to reflect their personal out-of-work interests)
-   Movie tickets

The range of options is endless and the range of costs is equally flexible. The important thing when you are rewarding the team is that they associate the reward with the effort.

If you wish to reward one or two people for an outstanding effort, personalize the rewards and let the others know why you have singled out the individuals. The team will place more value on the reward if you have put some thought and effort into it, rather than going for the easiest option.

But money can't be ignored

In the case of high achievers: Rewarding consistently high achievers is different from one off achievements. These ones need special care and their remuneration often needs adjusting to reflect their increasing value to the company.

In the case of steady performers: The vast majority of our staff will be steady performers. They need fair pay for their jobs and to have regular reviews of their pay. If they have done something special it is better to reward the specific event than to increase the pay because it can create expectation.

Chapter 9
The bottom line

Remember the formula

the Net Profit comes after expenses. Have a strategy for each part of this formula and never forget that your team's collective performance is the way you will achieve them

About the authors

Paul Watkins owned and franchised a group of video stores in the 1980s. He then headed up a regional tourism marketing organization for a decade before returning to retail. Paul has won awards for his marketing efforts and currently owns a pharmacy group with business partner Diego. Paul has authored three marketing books and is a sought after conference speaker.
paul@paulwatkins.co.nz

Diego Boniolo is a qualified pharmacist and owned his own retail pharmacy. After selling this to emigrate from South Africa, Diego set up and ran a 100-member pharmacy group. He currently co-owns and operates another pharmacy group with Paul.

Both authors has seen the good, the bad and the ugly of retail firsthand, so wrote the book after observing what works and what doesn't.

www.howsomeretailers.com